# Raising Clouded Leopards

Lisa MacDonald

Smithsonian

## Contributing Author

**Allison Duarte, M.A.**

## Consultants

**Tamieka Grizzle, Ed.D.**
*K–5 STEM Lab Instructor*
*Harmony Leland Elementary School*

**Jessica Kordell**
*Mammal Keeper*
*Smithsonian*

**Publishing Credits**

Rachelle Cracchiolo, M.S.Ed., *Publisher*
Conni Medina, M.A.Ed., *Managing Editor*
Diana Kenney, M.A.Ed., NBCT, *Content Director*
Véronique Bos, *Creative Director*
June Kikuchi, *Content Director*
Robin Erickson, *Art Director*
Seth Rogers, *Editor*
Mindy Duits, *Senior Graphic Designer*
Smithsonian Science Education Center

**Image Credits:** front cover, p.1 Kris Wiktor/Shutterstock; back cover, p.5 (bottom), p.8, p.20, p.21 (top), p.22, p.23, p.24, p.31 © Smithsonian; p.4 Andy Cross/The Denver Post via Getty Images; p.6 Imagemore Co, Ltd./Getty Images; p.7 (bottom) Joel Sartore/ National Geographic/Getty Images; p.9 Timothy Large/Alamy; p.12 Terry Whittaker/ Science Source; p.13 (bottom) Rich Carey/Shutterstock; p.14 volkerpreusser/Alamy; p.16 Bertrand Gardel / Hemis/Alamy; all other images from iStock and/or Shutterstock.

**Library of Congress Cataloging-in-Publication Data**

Names: MacDonald, Lisa, author.
Title: Raising Clouded leopards / Lisa MacDonald.
Description: Huntington Beach, CA : Teacher Created Materials, [2018] | Audience: K to grade 3. | Includes index.
Identifiers: LCCN 2017056315 (print) | LCCN 2017061252 (ebook) | ISBN 9781493869169 (e-book) | ISBN 9781493866762 (pbk.)
Subjects: LCSH: Clouded leopard--Juvenile literature. | Clouded leopard--Conservation--Juvenile literature. | Wildlife conservation--Juvenile literature.
Classification: LCC QL737.C23 (ebook) | LCC QL737.C23 M1655 2018 (print) | DDC 599.75--dc23
LC record available at https://lccn.loc.gov/2017056315

Smithsonian



**Teacher Created Materials**

5301 Oceanus Drive
Huntington Beach, CA 92649-1030
www.tcmpub.com

**ISBN 978-1-4938-6676-2**


Printed by: 590835
Printed in: China

# Table of Contents

# Not Your Average Cat

Look over there! Did you see the wild cat before it ran away? That cat is a clouded leopard. It is threatened, which means there are few of them left in the wild.

People want to find wild animals for different reasons. Some people want to keep them as rare pets. Some people hunt them. These actions are not safe for the animals or for people. Others hurt wild animals by accident. They ruin habitats, which can lead to the loss of food and places to live.

Other people want to find wild animals to help them. Scientists want to study clouded leopards. They hope to learn what clouded leopards need to survive. The more that is known, the more we can do to help them. But this is not easy since leopards are hard to find in the wild.

A Denver Zoo worker feeds a clouded leopard.

Construction workers tear down part of the Borneo rain forest, where clouded leopards live.

clouded leopard

# Meet Clouded Leopards

What do scientists know about clouded leopards? They are small for a "big" cat. They weigh between 11 and 23 kilograms (25 and 50 pounds). Their appearance gives clues about how they live. They have long tails and short legs compared to other wild cats. These **traits** give them good balance so they can climb trees.

Clouded leopards also have big paws with sharp claws. Their pads are flexible, and their rear ankles turn backward. These traits help them grip branches so they can climb down a tree headfirst!

## Special Sounds

Lions roar and house cats purr. Clouded leopards do neither. Instead, they growl, hiss, and **chuff**. Why do different cat **species** make different sounds? Differences in the bones and shape of a cat's throat change the sounds it can make.

pads on a clouded leopard paw

SCIENCE

## Open Wide

Clouded leopards have hinged jaws that allow them to open their mouths to 100-degree angles. That's four times wider than humans! This allows clouded leopards to eat larger animals.

clouded leopard yawning

## Private Cats

Not much is known about how clouded leopards live in the wild. But scientists are finding new ways to study them. Most wild cats like to be alone most of the time. Scientists think clouded leopards are solitary, too. Even leopards that live in the same region do not spend much time together.

## A Different Species

Animals' names say a lot about them. This is true for clouded leopards, too. The "clouded" part of their name comes from the pattern on their coats. The large spots look like clouds.

The "leopard" part is trickier. Some people might think that the clouded leopard is a type of leopard. Scientists now know that it is a completely different species. To understand what this means, think of a pug and a poodle. They are both dogs, but they are not the same type of dog. Now think of a pug and a wolf. They are different species.

TECHNOLOGY

## Camera Trapping

To find out how clouded leopards act when they are alone, scientists film them. Scientists build camera traps. They add sensors to cameras. When an animal moves past a sensor, *click!* It is "captured" on the camera. These images show how animals act in the wild.

# Clouded Leopards at Home

Clouded leopards live in Southeast Asia and the Eastern Himalayas. They are found as far south as Malaysia. They **adapt** to a wide range of habitats. Clouded leopards live in rain forests. They live in dry forests and swamps, too. They have been found both close to sea level and high in the mountains. All of these places have one thing in common—trees.

Clouded leopards spend a lot of time in trees. They track their **prey** from the branches. They also rest in trees during the day. Since they live in trees, they are called *arboreal* (ahr-BOHR-ee-uhl).

Some animals sleep at night and hunt during the day. Others do the opposite. Some scientists think that clouded leopards are mostly active at dusk and at dawn.

A clouded leopard looks for prey from a tree.

A group of clouded leopards is called a leap.

## People Problems

Clouded leopards live in forests. But people use forests, too. Trees are cut down to make lumber. They are also cut down to make room for buildings. When that happens, clouded leopards lose their homes. The small animals they eat are scared away. This means that the leopards will not have enough to eat.

People can cause other problems, too. Some hunt leopards for their spotted pelts. They capture them and sell them as pets, too. And they make medicine from the cats' claws and bones.

All of these things have caused the number of clouded leopards in the world to decrease. Taiwan used to have clouded leopards. Now, there are none left. People must do their part to help. No one wants these beautiful cats to become extinct.

clouded leopard pelts

Some people call clouded leopards "real-life Tiggers." They bounce from tree branch to tree branch.

Construction workers cut down trees for lumber in the Borneo rain forest.

# Helping or Hurting?

For clouded leopards to survive, they must be able to live and **breed** in the wild. The first step is to protect their habitat. One way to do this is to make their homes into wildlife preserves. These are places where people cannot build or hunt. Preserves keep animals safe.

In the case of clouded leopards, preserves have to be big enough to cover the **home ranges** of several cats. That is a lot of land. Problems arise if people want to cut down the trees in these areas for wood. Or, if people want to build homes on land in a clouded leopard's home range, there could be a fight for space.

A plan is needed. A good plan will work for people *and* clouded leopards. **Conservation** groups can help make those plans. They protect wildlife.

MATHEMATICS

## Calculating Home Range

How big are clouded leopards' homes in the wild? To find out, scientists put radio collars on some wild leopards. Then, they tracked where the cats went. They found the size of the area. Each clouded leopard's home is 26 to 39 square kilometers (10 to 15 square miles).

## Challenges and Successes

Clouded leopards can be found in more than one country. That means that no one nation can save them alone. To keep them safe, places must pass the same laws. But it can be hard to get people to agree. For instance, some countries let people hunt leopards. Others only let a small amount of hunting take place. And still others do not allow hunting at all. Having different laws makes things harder.

Some clouded leopards prey on goats and sheep that live on nearby farms. Farmers need to protect their **livestock**. So, they shoot the leopards that attack. To stop this, some groups have started paying farmers for the animals they lose. This plan has reduced the number of big cats killed each year.

Clouded leopards are called "tree tigers" in Malaysia.

Two women walk with a herd of goats.

## How Zoos Help

A lot of the research on clouded leopards has been done at zoos. So zoos work together and share what they know. This helps them learn more about leopards' needs.

Scientists want more clouded leopards in the world. Many zoos are part of breeding programs. These programs started with clouded leopards that were saved from poachers and illegal pet traders. It is hard to match wild leopards. When wild cats meet, it can be dangerous. They may fight. One of them may be hurt or killed.

Over time, researchers have thought of new ways to match clouded leopards. One solution is to have them meet while they are young. It is best if they are less than one year old. This makes them less likely to fight when they are adults. But this does not always mean they make good matches.

This clouded leopard climbs a tree in its enclosure.

ARTS

## Designing Habitats

At a zoo, it is not enough to make animal enclosures look pretty. Each one is designed to look like a natural habitat. For example, clouded leopards spend a lot of time in trees, so zoos put branches at many heights. To design a habitat, zoo staff need to study what each animal needs.

As breeding programs at zoos grow, more cubs will be born and raised. That means more cubs will grow up to have cubs of their own.

Smithsonian's National Zoo is now part of a successful breeding program. But it took a lot of hard work to make it that way. At first, many cubs did not survive. Scientists at the zoo needed help. They worked with researchers at two other zoos. One zoo is in Nashville, Tennessee. The other zoo is in Thailand. Together, they found out how to keep the cubs alive. The joint program has produced more than 70 cubs.

Thanks to zoos, scientists have learned some important things about what leopards need. They know the foods that are best for these cats. They know the space they need. They also know the types of toys leopards want to play with. All of this knowledge helps zoos take care of clouded leopards.

This two-month-old clouded leopard was bred at Smithsonian's National Zoo.

This cub drinks from a bottle.

Clouded leopards have long **canines**. Their teeth are the same size as a full-grown tiger's teeth!

## Hello, Baby

Female clouded leopards can have cubs when they are two years old. They are pregnant for about three months. Females usually have two or three cubs, but they may have up to five! Newborn cubs are tiny. They only weigh about 150 to 300 grams (5 to 10 ounces).

In zoos, cubs nurse until they are three months old. They stay with their mothers for a year and a half to two years. After that, they find mates and have cubs of their own.

Each clouded leopard cub is very important. That is why people hand-raise cubs at zoos. They are taken to a separate nursery to keep them safe.

Most cubs in zoos survive to adulthood. They are also more likely to have cubs of their own!

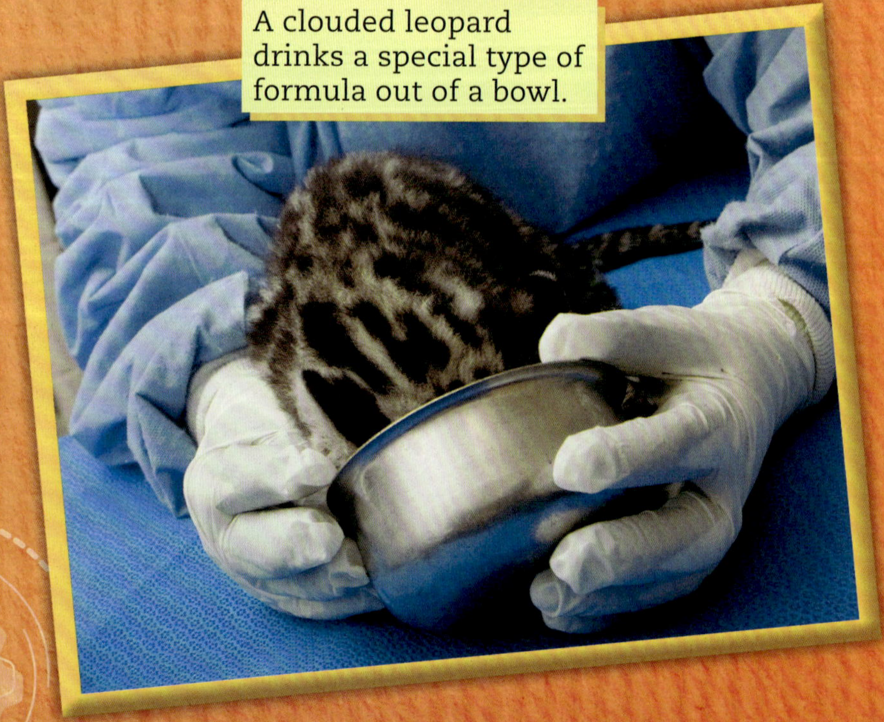

A clouded leopard drinks a special type of formula out of a bowl.

When a clouded leopard is born, it eats seven times per day! Zookeepers take turns feeding the cats.

Zoos have some years when a lot of cubs are born. But they also have years when no cubs are born. No cubs were born at the National Zoo for 15 years in a row. Then, in 2009, a cub named Ta Moon and his brother, Sa Ming, were born. The next year, two more cubs were born. Many more cubs have been born since then. Ta Moon is the father of four of them!

Scientists at the National Zoo help other zoos in their breeding programs. In 2015, a clouded leopard was born at the Nashville Zoo. His name is Niran. Scientists at the two zoos worked together to help Niran's mother become pregnant. Their work will help more clouded leopards have cubs at zoos.

These two cubs were born on February 14, 2010, at Smithsonian's National Zoo.

ENGINEERING

## Stress-Free Zoo Homes

When clouded leopards are stressed, it is hard for them to have cubs. So, staff at zoos make them specially designed homes. Since leopards are tree dwellers, tall objects for them to climb were built to make them feel safer. Keeping them away from other big cats helps, too.

# The Future Is Clouded

It's not too late to help clouded leopards. It took a long time to learn what these cats need in zoos and in the wild to survive. Now that we know, efforts to save them must continue.

A small group of people cannot fix this on their own. Scientists must learn more about clouded leopards to help them. Groups must fight for laws that protect cats' habitats. And animal lovers must share the story of clouded leopards. That way, the number of cats can keep increasing.

Everyone must work together. We must share information. That is the best way to help save clouded leopards. We can't give up!

# STEAM CHALLENGE

## Define the Problem

Your local zoo is starting a breeding program to help save the clouded leopard. You have been asked to design the new exhibit. How will you use what you have learned to make a zoo habitat for these animals?

**Constraints:** The exhibit must be able to house 4 clouded leopards at one time.

**Criteria:** A successful design will look like their natural habitat, make the animals feel safe, and allow scientists and visitors to observe them.

## 1 Research and Brainstorm

Look for information in the book about the life and behavior of clouded leopards. Do clouded leopards live in groups or alone? Do they need separate spaces? What do the animals like to do? How will the scientists watch the animals in your model?

## 2 Design and Build

Sketch your design of the exhibit. What purpose will each part serve? What materials will work best? Build the model.

## 3 Test and Improve

Your classmates will act as the zoo's scientists. Show and explain your model exhibit to the group. Ask for ways to improve the design. How will you use this information to make changes? Modify your design and present it again.

## 4 Reflect and Share

Do you think scientists share their work? What are some benefits of sharing ideas in science and engineering? How did you learn from others during this challenge?

# Glossary

**adapt**—to adjust to new conditions

**breed**—to mate and produce animal babies

**canines**—pointed teeth of a mammal

**chuff**—to make a sharp, puffing sound

**conservation**—the protection of natural resources

**extinct**—no longer existing

**home ranges**—areas over which animals or groups of animals regularly travel

**livestock**—farm animals raised for use and profit

**nurse**—to feed one's young with milk

**poachers**—people who hunt and kill animals illegally

**prey**—an animal being hunted, caught, and eaten by another animal

**solitary**—being or living alone or without companions

**species**—a group of plants or animals that are related and can produce young

**traits**—qualities and characteristics that make people or things different from others

# Index

# CAREER ADVICE

from Smithsonian

**Do you want to protect animals?**
**Here are some tips to get you started.**

*"Conserving animals takes all kinds of people working in all types of jobs. Photographer, teacher, animal keeper, policy maker, or writer—apply what you love to conservation." —**Jilian Fazio, Ph.D., Clouded Leopard Species Survival Plan Coordinator***

*"Start early and volunteer. Many organizations are looking for dedicated individuals to help out. Explore different avenues. This is your chance to try a job that sounds fun and find out if it really is! Be passionate, work hard, and take opportunities." —**Jessica Kordell, Mammal Keeper***